Original title:
The Recipe for Relational Resilience

Copyright © 2024 Swan Charm
All rights reserved.

Author: Johan Kirsipuu
ISBN HARDBACK: 978-9916-86-572-9
ISBN PAPERBACK: 978-9916-86-573-6
ISBN EBOOK: 978-9916-86-574-3

Kneading Moments Together

In the kitchen, warmth surrounds,
Flour and smiles, love abounds.
Hands together, kneading fate,
A dance of joy, we cultivate.

Laughter rises, the dough does too,
Sweet aromas, as dreams brew.
Side by side, our hearts align,
Creating memories, divine.

Rolling pins and playful fights,
Whisking hopes in cozy nights.
With every knead, a bond grows strong,
In this moment, we belong.

Seasons of Growth

Springtime whispers, a new dawn glows,
Nature awakens, as beauty grows.
Petals bloom where joy resides,
In the warmth, our love abides.

Summer paints with vibrant hues,
Basking in sun, we chase our views.
Moments cherished, laughter shared,
In the sun's embrace, we dared.

Autumn's palette, rich and warm,
Leaves falling gently, a golden charm.
Together we gather, hand in hand,
Harvest our dreams, just as we planned.

Cultivating Communication

Words as seeds, we gently sow,
Understanding helps us grow.
Through open hearts and listening ears,
We bridge the gaps, dissolve the fears.

In every dialogue, trust takes flight,
Guiding us through the darkest night.
Conversations bloom with every thought,
In this garden, love is sought.

With patience, we nurture, cultivate,
Intentions clear, we resonate.
Through shared stories, lives entwined,
In the heart's embrace, we find.

Spice of Spontaneity

In a moment, life can change,
A whispered plan, so strange,
Adventures call, we take the leap,
Into the unknown, memories to keep.

A road untraveled, laughter flows,
Surprise encounters, excitement grows.
In silly dances, we find delight,
With hearts ignited, spirits bright.

Each unplanned trip brings us near,
Moments cherished, oh so dear.
In spontaneity, love ignites,
Together we chase the endless nights.

Adventures in Connection

In a world where paths entwine,
Old friends gather, hearts align,
Whispers sweet as morning dew,
Every moment feels brand new.

Laughter echoes, stories shared,
In the bond, we are declared,
Across the miles, we still feel,
A tether strong, a vibrant reel.

From twilight talks to sunrise gleam,
In every glance, a silent beam,
We chase the stars, our dreams take flight,
In this dance, we find our light.

Through winding roads and stormy skies,
Together, we rise and brave the highs,
In every struggle, hand in hand,
United, we make our stand.

So let us wander, hearts ablaze,
In adventures shared, our spirits raise,
For in the journey, joy we find,
Connection's magic, truly kind.

The Table of Trust

Gathered 'round the wooden grain,
Each voice a note, a sweet refrain,
With open hearts, we share our tales,
In this space, no truth derails.

Candles flicker, warmth surrounds,
In laughter's glow, connection's found,
Every secret gently spoken,
In this trust, no hearts are broken.

Plates are filled, the feast of choice,
In every meal, we find our voice,
Moments savored, time stands still,
Together, we bend fate to will.

Through the silence, comfort grows,
In shared eyes, the love still shows,
From every burden, light is cast,
In trust's embrace, we hold steadfast.

So raise your glass, a bond we toast,
To friendships formed and memories most,
At this table, we all belong,
In the heart of trust, we're ever strong.

A Flavorful Commitment

In the garden, seeds we sow,
Promises whispered, soft and low.
Through weathered storms, we stand and cheer,
A blend of flavors, rich and clear.

Together we mix the sweet and sour,
Like rain and sun, we share the hour.
A recipe crafted with love and care,
Our hearts entwined, a bond so rare.

With every bite, the taste confirms,
In unity, our spirit warms.
A flavorful path we forge today,
In commitment true, we find our way.

Symbiotic Journeys

Two lives intertwine, a dance so fine,
Like vines that join, we intertwine.
Through ups and downs, through joy and pain,
In every heartbeat, love remains.

We share our burdens, lift the weight,
In trust and kindness, we create.
Each step we take, a lesson learned,
With every turn, our souls have burned.

The path we walk, it bends and sways,
In symbiosis, we find our ways.
Two hearts as one, we journey far,
Guided by hope, our guiding star.

A Symphony of Voices

In harmony, our voices rise,
A blend of dreams beneath the skies.
Each note a story, rich and bright,
Together, we ignite the night.

A chorus woven, warm and bold,
With every sound, a truth unfolds.
Diverse in tone, yet close in heart,
In unity, our song will start.

Echoes dance in the evening air,
A symphony of love, pure and rare.
With every phrase, we share our pain,
In every refrain, our joy's regained.

Balancing Differences

In contrast lies a beauty found,
Where opposites in balance sound.
Like night and day, they intertwine,
In every heartbeat, a sacred sign.

Embracing shades that set apart,
Both light and dark can heal a heart.
Each strength we bring, a gift to share,
Together, we thrive, a tender care.

In varied paths, we learn to see,
The art of love in harmony.
With hands held tight, we'll carve our way,
In balanced dance, forever stay.

Infusions of Love

In the pot, warmth swirls bright,
A blend of spices, pure delight.
Hearts embraced in every taste,
Moments shared, none go to waste.

Laughter dances in the air,
Each sip whispers, showing care.
A secret recipe we keep,
With every meal, our souls leap.

Stirring time with gentle hands,
Together in these culinary lands.
Love is simmered, rich and deep,
In every bite, our memories seep.

A Plate Full of Promise

On the table, colors gleam,
Hopes are stirred within a dream.
Each morsel tells a tale anew,
Of laughter shared, and friends so true.

Gathered 'round, we will explore,
Flavors knocking at the door.
A journey crafted, plate by plate,
With each fresh bite, we celebrate.

Textures mingle, joys collide,
Promise kept with each good side.
Together we carve out our space,
In every dish, we find our grace.

Authentic Ingredients

Freshly picked from garden's edge,
Nature's gifts, we make a pledge.
Savor the essence, pure and true,
In every dish, it shines right through.

Hand in hand, we chop and slice,
Crafting meals that feel so nice.
Herbs and roots, a fragrant blend,
With every bite, our spirits mend.

Cultivating love, one seed at time,
Honoring Nature, in rhythm, in rhyme.
Authenticity shines bright and clear,
In every taste, we hold you near.

Relishing Reliability

Comfort found in every bite,
Familiar tastes that feel so right.
A dish remembered, served with care,
In every meal, a love we share.

Through seasons change, we stand still,
Trusting tastes that always thrill.
Recipes passed from heart to heart,
In every kitchen, life's sweet art.

Moments cherished, day by day,
Together always, come what may.
Reliability on every plate,
With every meal, we celebrate.

Harmony in Chaos

In the whirlwind of life, we find,
A dance where the chaos unwinds.
Notes of laughter, tears interlace,
In the tumult, we find our place.

Stormy skies may drop their rage,
Yet beauty blooms on every page.
Within the madness, peace ignites,
Guiding souls towards the lights.

Voices clash like a thunderclap,
Yet in discord, we hear the map.
A cacophony turns to a song,
In our hearts, we all belong.

Through the noise, we learn to see,
Chaos carries a melody.
With every clash, a chance to grow,
Harmony's seeds begin to sow.

Together we rise, united and tall,
In chaos, we'll find the call.
Embrace the storm, dance in the rain,
For in harmony, joy will reign.

Cultivating Kindness

In small gestures, kindness blooms,
Lighting up the darkest rooms.
A gentle smile, a helping hand,
In every heart, we'd understand.

Words like seeds, we plant with care,
Nurturing love, we all can share.
Compassion flows like a river wide,
In the warmth, our hopes abide.

As flowers turn towards the sun,
Let our kindness never shun.
In every act, the grace we show,
Our spirits rise, and love will grow.

With listening hearts, we can embrace,
Everyone deserves a sacred space.
In this garden, let us thrive,
Together, we keep kindness alive.

For in each soul, a spark we find,
Creating bridges, heart entwined.
As we flourish, hand in hand,
A world of kindness, we'll expand.

Marinating in Patience

In the stillness, time unfolds,
Life's true treasures are not so bold.
A gentle breath, a mindful pause,
In patience, we find our cause.

Seasons change at their own pace,
Growth is often a quiet grace.
In the waiting, wisdom grows,
Nature teaches what patience knows.

Like a river carving stone,
Patience whispers, we are not alone.
Through each trial, calmness finds,
The beauty in unhurried minds.

Counting moments, one by one,
Under the watchful, patient sun.
Every heartbeat, a lesson learned,
In still waters, our dreams are churned.

With open hearts, we take the lead,
Trust the journey, plant the seed.
For in the waiting, life will flow,
Marinating in patience, we learn to grow.

The Art of Listening

In a world that often shouts,
Let us listen, clear our doubts.
Every voice has a tale untold,
Wrapped in wisdom, bright and bold.

With open ears and hearts so true,
We embrace the stories coming through.
A quiet nod, a soft reply,
In the silence, we learn to fly.

Caring presence, a gentle guide,
In the rhythm, we take pride.
Each word spoken, a fragile thread,
We weave connections, hearts widespread.

Listening deep, we find the grace,
To understand another's space.
In every silence, we find a song,
The art of listening helps us belong.

In the tapestry of life we spin,
Together, let the healing begin.
For in every heart, a story waits,
Through listening, we unlock the gates.

Harmony in a Chaotic Kitchen

Amidst the clatter, pots collide,
Flavors mingle, dreams reside.
A dash of laughter, a hint of grace,
In this chaos, we find our place.

Sizzle of onions, the garlic's song,
Ingredients dance, where we belong.
Sharing stories, cutting through time,
In the chaos, our hearts align.

A sprinkle of patience, a stir of love,
Gathering strength from the sky above.
Together we cook, together we grow,
In this kitchen, our spirits glow.

The aroma rises, we take a seat,
With every bite, life tastes sweet.
From chaos, a symphony we create,
Harmony found on each plate.

As dishes empty, laughter remains,
In our hearts, the warmth sustains.
Chaos may reign, but through it all,
United we stand, we never fall.

Spice of Empathy

A pinch of kindness, a sprinkle of care,
In every moment, let hearts declare.
Listen closely, let silence speak,
In shared silence, it's love we seek.

The heat of anger, the chill of doubt,
Empathy brews, we figure it out.
Stirring connections, flavors embrace,
In understanding, we find our place.

Conversations simmer, simmering thoughts,
Thread of compassion, the fabric is wrought.
We gather wisdom, taste life's stew,
For the spice of empathy is what pulls us through.

A warm embrace when words are few,
In this connection, we find what's true.
We share our stories, we savor and blend,
With every encounter, our hearts will mend.

May we add spice to the lives we touch,
In every gesture, we care so much.
Through trials and triumphs, hand in hand,
The spice of empathy, forever we stand.

The Alchemy of Connection

A tender moment, a thread so fine,
In the fabric of life, our hearts entwine.
Each shared glance, a spark ignites,
Transforming shadows into bright lights.

Laughter echoes, weaving through space,
In the alchemy, we find our grace.
Transforming sorrow, joy we create,
With every bond, we resonate.

Conversations flow like rivers deep,
In silence shared, our souls we keep.
With every heart, a piece we share,
The magic of connection fills the air.

Moments treasured like gold that gleams,
Each connection crafted from our dreams.
United in purpose, attitudes sway,
In the alchemy of life, we play.

As we gather 'round, let spirits soar,
Within the connection, we're never poor.
In the pot of togetherness, we blend,
The alchemy of love will never end.

Savoring Shared Moments

Pause for a moment, breathe in the day,
Savor the sweetness, come what may.
Every heartbeat, a story unfolds,
In these shared moments, our life molds.

With friends around, laughter ignites,
Filling the air with pure delights.
Taste of nostalgia, flavors entwined,
In each bite, the past we find.

Time slows down, in the stillness we gleam,
Building connections, living the dream.
With every toast, our spirits align,
Celebrating together, a moment divine.

A tapestry woven with love and care,
Savoring life, with time to spare.
In every glance, a memory is made,
In shared moments, our hearts cascade.

So let's cherish these times, both bitter and sweet,
In this journey of life, let's make it complete.
As we hold each other close, let's never forget,
Savoring shared moments, our greatest asset.

Filling the Cup of Closeness

In the quiet moments shared,
Laughter dances in the air.
Hearts entwined, a gentle bond,
Together here, we are so strong.

Every glance, a silent vow,
In this space, we make the now.
Hand in hand, through time we flow,
Building dreams, our spirits glow.

With every word, a thread is spun,
Weaving tales of what's begun.
In this cup, our warmth we pour,
Filling it, forevermore.

A sip of trust, a dash of grace,
In this moment, find your place.
As shadows fade, the light we share,
Filling the cup with love and care.

Together we'll embrace the day,
In the joy, we find our way.
Through trials faced, we softly soar,
Filling the cup, forevermore.

Toasts to Turbulent Times

Raise a glass to storms we've faced,
In the chaos, courage traced.
With every tremble, hearts ignite,
Together strong, we find the light.

Through the trials, we have grown,
In our bond, we've found a home.
A toast to all the battles fought,
In the struggle, lessons taught.

Lift your spirits, don't despair,
In the shadows, love will spare.
With every toast, we gather round,
In turbulent times, strength is found.

We'll weather storms and dance through rain,
In our laughter, ease the pain.
To safer shores, we raise our voice,
In unity, we make the choice.

So here's to hopes yet to unfold,
In the warmth, we break the cold.
Together, through thick and thin,
Toasting life, let's start again.

Stirring Up Strength

In the hearth, we find the spark,
Stirring courage from the dark.
With each heartbeat, rise we do,
Strength is born from all we've been through.

Together, we blend our dreams,
In the warmth, hope brightly beams.
Stirring kindness, love, and care,
In this pot, we have our share.

With every challenge, we embrace,
Stirring up strength, finding grace.
In the heat of life's great test,
We rise, united, at our best.

Mixing laughter, a pinch of tears,
Creating memories through the years.
With every spoonful, joy we find,
Stirring bonds that gently bind.

So we gather, hearts in sync,
Stirring up courage, don't let it sink.
In this moment, we stand tall,
Stirring strength, we'll never fall.

The Taste of Togetherness

In the kitchen, scents collide,
Flavors dance, hearts open wide.
With every bite, a story told,
The taste of love will never grow old.

Gathered 'round the festive table,
In each dish, memories stable.
A sprinkle of laughter, a dash of cheer,
The taste of togetherness, always near.

From sweet to savory, we explore,
With open hearts, we find much more.
With every meal, we sow the seeds,
Of cherished moments, heart's great needs.

Through every season, flavors shift,
Cooking up love, the perfect gift.
To taste together, a feast divine,
In harmony, our lives intertwine.

So let's raise a glass to love,
A melody sent from above.
In every morsel, find the bliss,
The taste of togetherness, we won't miss.

The Embrace of Understanding

In shadows deep, we find a light,
A whispered truth in the quiet night.
Hearts open wide, they start to mend,
In gentle arms, we learn to bend.

Words flow soft like a tender stream,
Where empathy dances, and souls gleam.
In the silence, we hear the call,
To lift each other, to rise and fall.

With every heartbeat, we touch the core,
A bridge of trust, forevermore.
As we share the weight, we unearth grace,
In the warm embrace, we find our place.

Not just in sorrow, but joy we share,
In every moment, with love laid bare.
The world recedes, just you and me,
Together we write our symphony.

So take my hand, let's walk this way,
In each other's light, we choose to stay.
With open hearts, we venture new,
In the embrace of understanding, we break through.

The Heat of Unity

In the blaze of stars, we stand aligned,
Hearts beating strong, in spirit entwined.
Together we rise, our voices roar,
In the heat of unity, we ignite the floor.

Chains of division, we shatter and break,
In this fierce flame, we choose to awake.
With hands joined tight, we weather the storm,
In the heat of unity, we build and warm.

Each heartbeat echoes, strong and bold,
Together we gather, our stories unfold.
In the fire's glow, our fears dissolve,
In the heat of unity, we evolve.

Though paths may wander, and trials arise,
Through every struggle, our spirits will rise.
In the heat of unity, we trust and believe,
A tapestry woven, we will achieve.

So let us rise, let us proclaim,
In the heat of unity, we are the same.
Bound by our passion, our hopes in sight,
Together we shine—our future ignites.

Whipping Up Hope

In a bowl of dreams, we stir with care,
Each ingredient mixed is a wish to share.
A sprinkle of laughter, a dash of cheer,
Whipping up hope in the atmosphere.

As we fold in kindness, blend in grace,
Every heartbeat quickens, every space.
With flavors of joy, both sweet and bright,
Whipping up hope, we chase the night.

In this recipe, we find our way,
Guided by the love in what we say.
A pinch of courage, a splash of trust,
Whipping up hope, it's a must.

Like rising dough, we lift and grow,
In unity's warmth, we cultivate flow.
The oven's heat brings dreams to life,
Whipping up hope, we conquer strife.

So gather around, let's bake our dreams,
In this kitchen of life, let's share our themes.
For in every bite, in each gentle scoop,
We find our purpose—whipping up hope!

Steeping in Care

In the quiet corner, where moments pause,
Tea leaves unfurl with each gentle cause.
In boiling waters, the flavors blend,
Steeping in care, as we slowly mend.

With every steep, patience defines,
The warmth of hearts, where love entwines.
In fragrant whispers, we find our way,
Steeping in care, come what may.

As the sunlight streams through tender leaves,
In shared silence, the spirit believes.
In cups of kindness, we find our fate,
Steeping in care, together we create.

In gentle swirls, the world feels right,
As we sip slowly, savoring light.
Each droplet blessed, each moment rare,
Steeping in care, we lay our prayer.

So gather, dear friends, in this space we share,
Let us nourish our souls, show that we care.
In every essence, there's hope to declare,
In the art of love, steeping in care.

Carving Out Space

In the chaos of the day,
We seek a quiet place.
A corner draped in dreams,
Where thoughts softly lace.

Time turns gently here,
With whispers in the air.
We carve out moments sweet,
A bond beyond compare.

The world may rush on by,
Yet we remain so still.
In our sacred space,
Love's echoes gently thrill.

Each laugh a timeless mark,
Each sigh a vibrant trace.
In every shared heartbeat,
We find our perfect space.

So here we sit and breathe,
In shadows kissed by light.
Together, we are whole,
In peace, the world feels right.

The Sweet and Savory of Us

Like sugar on the tongue,
Your laugh is pure delight.
With each glance, I taste joy,
In the warmth of our night.

Savory moments dance,
In kitchens filled with light.
We stir our dreams together,
As the stars shine bright.

Spices blend in harmony,
A recipe unique.
Every flavor tells a tale,
Of love in every peak.

The table set for two,
With laughter as our bread.
In every bite we share,
There's a world that we've bred.

So let's savor this life,
With every dish we make.
In each sweet and savory,
The bond we'll never break.

Layers of Togetherness

In the fabric of our days,
We weave our stories tight.
Each layer tells a tale,
Of laughter, love, and light.

From the thinnest threads we start,
Building up our dreams.
Colors blend and swirl,
In the softest seams.

With every fold, we grow,
In strength, in joy, in trust.
Together we are rich,
In layers, love is just.

Through storms and sunny days,
We stitch our hearts in song.
In this patchwork of our lives,
Together we belong.

So let's embrace our quilt,
The warmth of us entwined.
In every layer of love,
A treasure we will find.

The Fire of Friendship

A spark ignites the night,
With laughter filling air.
We gather round the flame,
In moments that we share.

Stories light our hearts,
Like stars against the dark.
Each whispered secret glows,
As embers leave their mark.

Through trials and through joys,
We stoke this vibrant fire.
In friendship's warm embrace,
We find what we desire.

The flicker shows our strength,
In shadows, we stand tall.
Together, we are fierce,
The brightest flames of all.

So here's to every spark,
To bonds that never tire.
In the fire of friendship,
Our souls forever inspire.

Flourishing Through Storms

In the midst of raging skies,
Roots dig deep, they never sigh.
Braving winds that howl and scream,
Blooms emerge, they dare to dream.

Lessons learned from darkest nights,
Hope ignites with morning lights.
Strength is found in every tear,
While the heart begins to steer.

Yet the thunder does not cease,
Finding solace brings us peace.
Calm inside a tempest's fray,
Finding joy in each new day.

When the storm begins to wane,
Sunlight kisses, breaks the chain.
New beginnings start to rise,
Life reborn, a sweet surprise.

Embrace the chaos, take the chance,
Nature's choir sings and prance.
Flourishing through trials faced,
In each struggle, beauty traced.

Recipes for Unbreakable Ties

Mix a cup of trust and care,
A dash of laughter, always share.
Stir in memories, warm and bright,
Season with kindness, pure delight.

Gather friends around the flame,
Each voice adds to the same sweet name.
Taste the love in every bite,
Strength grows strong, our spirits light.

Crush the doubts and fears apart,
Fold in dreams to make a start.
Let the warmth of bonds unite,
As we savor the sweet night.

Simmer stories, let them blend,
A pot of friendship without end.
Life's dishes served with care,
Each helping made to fully share.

Preserve the moments, keep them close,
In this recipe, we'll engross.
For in the kitchen, hearts entwine,
Together forever, your hand in mine.

The Art of Being Present

Time will race, but we will stay,
Mind and heart in bright array.
Savor each and every breath,
In this moment, life feels fresh.

Listen closely, hear the sound,
Of laughter lost, yet always found.
A gentle touch, a knowing glance,
In stillness lies a sacred dance.

Nature speaks in whispers soft,
The world unfolds, we drift aloft.
With each heartbeat, turn the page,
Life's a canvas, we engage.

Let the present guide your way,
Hold it close, don't let it stray.
In every second, love will kiss,
An endless well of timeless bliss.

Embrace the now, let worries cease,
In every moment, find your peace.
The art of being here, alive,
In this moment, we truly thrive.

Cooking with Compassion

Gather 'round, the table set,
A warm embrace, we won't forget.
Chop the veggies, bright and bold,
With gentle hands, a heart of gold.

Stir the pot with love and care,
A recipe of joys to share.
Season kindness in each layer,
Nourishing souls, a loving prayer.

Taste the flavors, rich and sweet,
In every bite, our spirits meet.
Creating bonds with every dish,
Compassion served, a heartfelt wish.

Break the bread, let laughter flow,
Hearts entwined in every show.
Cooking comforts, brings us near,
In unity, we conquer fear.

As we dine, our stories blend,
Creating warmth that has no end.
Cooking with love, we rise above,
In every meal, we share our love.

Cooking Up Collaboration

In the kitchen we unite,
Mixing dreams with delight,
Gathered close, hands in motion,
A recipe born of devotion.

Ingredients blend with care,
Ideas rise, light as air,
Stirring thoughts in a pot,
Creating warmth, a shared plot.

Each pinch of trust we find,
Hearts and minds intertwined,
Flavors dance, we ignite,
Cooking up joy, pure and bright.

Chopping doubts, we prepare,
Yielding strength, a sweet flair,
Savoring each shared bite,
Together, we take flight.

In this feast of our making,
Connections bloom, no faking,
Together, we share our dreams,
A collaboration of gleams.

Baking in Vulnerability

Flour dusts the quiet space,
Hearts laid bare, we embrace,
Dough kneaded with our fears,
Courage rises with the years.

Each ingredient a piece of soul,
Whisking comfort, making whole,
Butter melts, a tender touch,
In this warmth, we are much.

Oven's heat, a gentle glow,
Learning in the ebb and flow,
As layers build, we disclose,
Baking truths as the warmth grows.

Freshly baked, we stand tall,
Holding close, we embrace all,
Sharing crumbs of our heart,
In this space, we won't part.

So let's savor what we share,
In this moment, laid so bare,
Baking dreams, hand in hand,
Grounded firm, together we stand.

The Sweetness of Resilience

In the garden, seeds take flight,
Through the dark, they find the light,
Beneath the soil, roots dig deep,
Growing strong, our hopes we keep.

Petals bloom, colors bright,
In the storm, we find our might,
With every bruise, a lesson learned,
A flame inside, forever burned.

Honey drips from trials faced,
In the struggle, sweetness placed,
With every tear, a chance to see,
Resilience flows, wild and free.

We rise again, no fear in sight,
With courage as our guiding light,
In the fight, we find our songs,
In unity, we all belong.

The sweetness of life's embrace,
A journey shared at our own pace,
Together strong, we stand so true,
Through every storm, we'll break through.

Foundations of Endurance

Beneath the ground, roots weave tight,
Holding fast through day and night,
Brick by brick, we build our dreams,
Laying paths, stitching seams.

Endurance thrives in every heart,
A promise made, a vital part,
Through the trials, we stand bold,
Each setback a story told.

With every struggle, we grow strong,
In the chorus, we belong,
Voices lifted, hands entwined,
In unity, our hopes aligned.

Hope is a foundation laid,
In the light, our fears betrayed,
Together, we face what's ahead,
In resilience, love is bred.

Building towers that touch the sky,
Together, we reach high and high,
With every heart, brick on the ground,
In this strength, our peace is found.

The Blend of Laughter and Tears

In shadows cast by moonlight bright,
We weave our stories, day and night.
Laughter dances, tears may fall,
Together we rise, together we call.

Through trials faced and joy embraced,
Life's melody, a thrilling chase.
A quilt of memories, stitched with care,
In every stitch, love lingers there.

With every smile that lights the way,
In every tear, a bright array.
We find our strength, a bond so dear,
In the blend of laughter, we persevere.

Life's bittersweet, a sacred art,
With open arms, we play our part.
From every heartbeat, we shall learn,
In every lesson, the heart will yearn.

We cherish moments, fleeting, rare,
In the stillness, we find each other there.
In laughter's glow and tears that gleam,
Together forever, we dare to dream.

Meal of Memories

Gathered 'round the table's grace,
Stories shared in every space.
The scent of spices fills the air,
Each dish a tale, crafted with care.

From laughter's echo to sorrow's sigh,
A feast where moments never die.
With every bite, a memory shared,
In flavors rich, our hearts are bared.

As plates are passed, connections grow,
In every morsel, love will flow.
The meal is warm, the hearts are too,
In this tapestry, it's me and you.

Through seasons change and time's embrace,
The table holds our sacred space.
Each meal a chapter, bold and bright,
In memories feasted, day and night.

Together we savor, never rush,
Moments linger, hearts in hush.
In each delicious, shared delight,
We nourish love, our endless light.

Nourishing the Soul Together

In gentle whispers, hearts connect,
A bond so deep, we can't reject.
With every glance, the world fades away,
In shared stillness, we find our way.

Through winding paths and distant skies,
We gather strength while dreaming high.
In quiet moments, laughter streams,
In nurturing souls, we chase our dreams.

Each gesture small, yet speaks so loud,
No need for masks; we stand unbowed.
With hands entwined, we face the storm,
In unity's warmth, we find our form.

Together we gather, seeds of grace,
In every heartbeat, a sacred space.
Through joy and pain, we learn and grow,
Nourishing the soul, love's gentle flow.

In twilight's embrace, we'll find our truth,
Holding on to cherished youth.
Together we rise, with hearts so bright,
Nourished by love, our guiding light.

Hand in Hand, Heart to Heart

With hands entwined, we start the dance,
In every step, a chosen chance.
Through hills and valleys, side by side,
In life's adventure, together we glide.

Each heartbeat echoes a timeless song,
In unity's strength, we both belong.
Hand in hand, we face the tide,
In heart to heart, there's nothing to hide.

Through storms that crash and winds that howl,
We stand as one, fierce and proud.
With trust as our shield and love as our guide,
Together we journey, hearts open wide.

In moments of stillness, we pause and breathe,
In every blessing, we find reprieve.
Hand in hand, our spirits soar,
In heart's embrace, forevermore.

Together we dream, and together we dare,
Through life's tapestry, a love so rare.
Hand in hand, heart to heart,
In every ending, there's a brand new start.

Culinary Connections

In the kitchen, spices dance,
Mixing flavors, a sweet romance.
Chopping vegetables, laughter flows,
In every bite, love surely grows.

Gather 'round the table bright,
Sharing stories, hearts in flight.
The warmth of broth, a soulful blend,
In every meal, we find a friend.

Sizzling pans, the aroma strong,
Binding us where we belong.
With every taste, a tale unfolds,
In every dish, a memory holds.

From humble meals to grand feasts,
Each recipe, a love that never ceases.
A pinch of joy, a dash of care,
In every forkful, we gladly share.

Culinary art, a bond so fine,
In every bite, your heart meets mine.
Together we savor, together we strive,
In our culinary world, we truly thrive.

Baking Common Ground

The oven hums with gentle heat,
Flour dust settles under our feet.
Kneading dough, we shape our dreams,
In every rise, our spirit beams.

Sugar and spice, the perfect blend,
Baking brings us closer, friend.
Rolling pin glides with steady grace,
In every cookie, a warm embrace.

Whisking eggs, our laughter stirs,
Filling the air, sweet scents confer.
From batter poured to cookies baked,
In each warm treat, love is staked.

Softened butter and chocolate chips,
Moments shared through tasty trips.
The joy of baking, hearts aligned,
Creating treats, our souls intertwined.

As aroma wafts, we gather near,
With every bite, we share our cheer.
In the art of baking, bonds are crowned,
Together, we find our common ground.

Crumbs of Compassionate Conversations

On a park bench, crumbs we share,
Stories woven within the air.
A gentle breeze speaks tales of old,
In every morsel, warmth unfolds.

Pastries shared with kindness true,
Every bite brings me closer to you.
The laughter echoes, rich and warm,
In these crumbs, we find our form.

With every sip of tea, we see,
Depth in conversations, set us free.
The world slows down, our hearts align,
Between the bites, your soul meets mine.

Nibbles exchanged, compassion reigns,
Healing moments, erasing pains.
Each crumb holds a secret, a spark,
Guiding us gently through the dark.

Underneath the vast, open sky,
In the simplest bites, we learn to fly.
Compassion thrives as we converse,
In each crumb shared, the universe.

Infusions of Intimacy

Teas and brews, aromas swirl,
In every cup, our hearts unfurl.
Steeping gently, passions blend,
In each sip, we transcend.

Boiling water, whispers soft,
Between us, emotions loft.
Herbal notes and fragrant spice,
In every taste, our love is nice.

Chilled glass teas under summer sun,
Moments shared, two become one.
With every pour, our spirits sigh,
In these infusions, we learn to fly.

From cozy chats to silent dreams,
In every brew, intimacy gleams.
Flavors mingle, our souls ignite,
In this ritual, love feels right.

Gathered close, our fingers touch,
Sipping slowly, we cherish each clutch.
In this dance of warmth and glee,
Infusions of intimacy, you and me.

Bonds Forged in Trust

In shadows deep, we found our light,
With whispered dreams, our hearts took flight.
Through storms we weathered, hand in hand,
A promise held, a sacred strand.

With every tear, our spirits grew,
In laughter shared, the trust we knew.
Like roots entwined beneath the ground,
In silent strength, true bonds are found.

Through trials faced and fears awoke,
In every silence, unspoken yoke.
Together we rise, together we stand,
Bound by the ties of love well-planned.

When shadows fall and doubts may creep,
Our faith in each other runs so deep.
In every heartbeat, a promise rings,
In the dance of life, our trust takes wings.

A journey marked by paths we choose,
With every step, we learn, we lose.
Yet through it all, our hearts remain,
In bonds forged, there's no space for pain.

Ingredients of Togetherness

A pinch of kindness, a dash of grace,
Mix in the laughter, brightens the space.
Stir in the memories, sweet and bold,
The warmth of stories, together told.

Sprinkle compassion, let it rise high,
Blend in respect, like clouds in the sky.
Fold in the moments, both big and small,
In the mix of life, we find our call.

Like spices dancing in a pot,
Each element adds, like it or not.
For togetherness thrives on love's embrace,
Creating a bond nothing can trace.

A dash of patience, a hearty cheer,
Taste of support when shadows appear.
The recipe's simple, yet oh so true,
With each ingredient, I'm drawn to you.

In friendships baked, we find our worth,
A table set, where love gives birth.
With every gathering, we add a new blend,
In the heart of togetherness, our souls transcend.

The Alchemy of Friendship

In the crucible of shared delight,
We forge our bonds in the soft moonlight.
With trust as the fire, we melt away,
The barriers that once led us astray.

Each smile a catalyst, pure and bright,
Transforming our fears into sheer delight.
Together we nurture, together we grow,
In the garden of friendship, love's seeds we sow.

With laughter's elixir and joy as our goal,
We shape each moment, the heart and the soul.
Through trials and triumphs, we find our way,
In the alchemy of friendship, we forever stay.

A bond that transcends the mundane grind,
In the melting pot, our lives combined.
With each memory forged, our spirits entwine,
In this precious concoction, your heart is mine.

In every heartbeat, the magic ignites,
Turning the ordinary into pure delights.
Though the world may change, one thing is clear,
In the alchemy of friendship, we'll conquer the fear.

Spice of Empathy

In the rich tapestry of heart and soul,
Empathy weaves, makes us whole.
A sprinkle of kindness, a thoughtful glance,
In the dance of connection, we find our chance.

With every story shared, we deepen the ties,
Seeing through others' hearts and eyes.
In the flavor of understanding, we savor the sound,
Of voices united, compassion unbound.

Like spices that mingle, diverse yet one,
Empathy blooms under the warmth of the sun.
As we breathe in the world, our hearts start to blend,
In the spice of empathy, we find our true friend.

With every gesture, our hearts engage,
Navigating life, page by page.
In the silence of knowing, we share a breath,
Embracing the stories, even those of death.

As seasons change and moments flow,
The essence of empathy continues to grow.
With each life touched, a tapestry spun,
In the spice of empathy, we are all one.

The Warmth of Togetherness

In the glow of shared laughter,
Hearts open wide and free.
Together we face each chapter,
Creating our own harmony.

Hands intertwined, we stand strong,
Weathering storms side by side.
In each other's arms, we belong,
Together, our spirits abide.

Through the darkness, we find light,
Guiding each other through strife.
With each moment, pure delight,
Together, we celebrate life.

Trust is the root of our bond,
In unity, we find our grace.
In each memory, we're fond,
Together, we embrace our space.

The warmth that we share will grow,
In every heartbeat, a song.
With love's embrace, we all glow,
Together is where we belong.

The Essence of Teamwork

United we strive, hand in hand,
Each role distinct, yet combined.
In this effort, we make our stand,
Dreams and goals intertwined.

Voices rise as one in cheer,
Celebrating each little win.
Together we conquer our fear,
In sync, we begin again.

Every challenge brings us close,
Our strengths shine through the night.
In collaboration, we chose,
To transform dark into light.

A tapestry woven tight,
Each thread tells a story near.
In teamwork, we find our might,
Together, we'll overcome fear.

With every step, we move forth,
Energized by shared intent.
In this journey of true worth,
Together, our lives are spent.

Harvesting Shared Dreams

In the field where hopes are sown,
We gather each seed with care.
Together, we've brightly grown,
Dreams nurtured in open air.

With every sunrise, we rise,
Tending to our shared delight.
In unity, we realize,
Our vision shines pure and bright.

The fruits of our labor so sweet,
Bonds forged through trust and time.
In this journey, we compete,
Yet celebrate every climb.

As we gather in the eve,
Stories of our growth unfold.
Together, we all believe,
In dreams that are woven gold.

Hand in hand, we reap the good,
Fostering a brighter way.
In our hearts, it's understood,
Together, we'll seize the day.

Notes of Connection

In quiet whispers, we share,
Soft melodies through the air.
Each note a bridge, a soft prayer,
In silence, we show we care.

Eyes that meet, reflecting truth,
In the rhythm of gentle sighs.
Moments freeze, reclaiming youth,
In the music, our spirit flies.

Through every beat, hearts align,
Creating a symphony here.
Together, we craft the design,
Filling the voids with sheer cheer.

In laughter's song, we find peace,
Every heartbeat a shared refrain.
Through shared moments, joy won't cease,
In connection, we break the chain.

As the melody fades away,
Our connection lingers still.
In these notes, our hearts will stay,
Together, we find our will.

Flavors of Forgiveness

Bitter thoughts soften with time,
Sweet moments linger, they chime.
Sour regrets fade away slow,
A sprinkle of kindness helps grow.

Salty tears wash away pain,
In the heart, love will remain.
Savory lessons emerge bright,
Forgiveness, a guiding light.

Fruits of patience, ripe and true,
Yet every flavor tells our view.
In the pot, we stir and blend,
A taste of peace, hearts mend.

Cups of empathy brim full,
Gentle hearts, tender, and dull.
Savoring all that has passed,
Together in this feast, we last.

Each bite a story, a song,
In forgiveness, we all belong.
Flavors mix, and we embrace,
In this banquet, find our place.

The Fusion of Memories

Old photographs whisper tales,
Laughter echoing, love prevails.
Sunset skies painted with dreams,
In the silence, memory gleams.

Moments frozen in time's grasp,
Held closely, in nostalgia, clasp.
Childhood wonders, soft and bright,
Together they dance in the light.

Mixing colors of heart and mind,
Treasured snippets of humankind.
Faded pages, stories told,
In each chapter, we find gold.

Scent of familiar embraces,
Lingering smiles in warm spaces.
Taste of joy, pinch of sorrow,
A tapestry woven for tomorrow.

In a cauldron of what was real,
Memories blend, they help us heal.
Every smile, every tear shared,
In this fusion, we're all bared.

Sifting through Struggles

In the shadows, trials creep,
Heavy burdens, thoughts run deep.
Through the chaos, we must sift,
Finding meaning in each rift.

Like sand through the fingers flow,
Lessons hide where hard winds blow.
Picking grains of hope and pain,
In the storm, we learn to gain.

Each struggle shapes us inside,
Against the current, we must bide.
Emerging stronger, through the fray,
Life's a dance, come what may.

With every stumble, we rise tall,
In the silence, hear the call.
Sifting through what's lost and scarred,
Finding strength where hearts are marred.

In the end, we find our worth,
Every struggle brings rebirth.
Hand in hand with fears we fight,
Through the darkness, we find light.

Mixing Emotions

A splash of joy meets deep despair,
Colors swirl, and hearts lay bare.
Anger ignites, then fades away,
In this whirlpool, we all sway.

Love bubbles up, a soft embrace,
Fear dims but then finds its place.
Excitement dances, hope takes flight,
In the blend of day and night.

Tears flow freely, laughter bright,
Every hue, a borrowed light.
In the palette, we find our tune,
Painting dreams under the moon.

Swirling feelings, never still,
Each emotion shapes our will.
With every pulse, with every beat,
The mix of life feels bittersweet.

In this cocktail of the soul,
We drink deep, seeking to be whole.
Every sip tells a story clear,
In the mixing, we find cheer.

The Journey of a Thousand Meals.

From kitchen flames, aromas rise,
Each spice a tale, each dish a prize.
Gathered around the table's glow,
We share our hearts, let stories flow.

Forks clink softly, laughter rings,
In every bite, a joy that sings.
With every recipe, a bond we weave,
In food, we find what we believe.

Through seasons' change, we cook and share,
Reminders of love, the warmth we wear.
Each meal a chapter, each taste a smile,
Cultures unite, if just for a while.

Together we savor, together we learn,
In every meal, a page we turn.
From pot to plate, the essence flows,
Through journeys vast, our spirit grows.

So here's to meals, both small and grand,
That nourish the soul and help us stand.
In the journey through flavors, we find our way,
Together in connection, come what may.

Sustaining Connections

In quiet moments, hands entwined,
We build the bridges, close the binds.
Each word a seed, each smile a space,
Growing together at a gentle pace.

Friendships flourish, roots run deep,
In shared laughter, our sorrows seep.
Through trials faced, through joys we find,
Sustaining bonds, heart and mind.

Weathered days, yet still we stand,
Supporting each other, hand in hand.
With open hearts, we give and take,
In every moment, connections make.

Beneath the stars, we gather round,
In whispered secrets, love is found.
Through changing tides and shifting sand,
The ties between us, forever grand.

So cherish the ties that time won't sever,
In this life's journey, let's connect forever.
With paths entwined, let's face the light,
In sustaining connections, our hearts take flight.

Threads of Understanding

Across the world, each thread we weave,
With different colors, we learn to believe.
In stories shared, we find the truth,
A tapestry rich, from the heart of youth.

In eyes that shine, in minds that seek,
We grasp the lessons, the strong and weak.
With open hearts, we challenge the fray,
Threads of understanding light the way.

In moments of silence, and gestures bold,
In every encounter, new truths unfold.
Acknowledging differences, we find our voice,
In unity's strength, we make the choice.

In shared experience, we bridge the gap,
A fabric of life, a vibrant map.
Through kindness given and wisdom earned,
Threads of understanding, forever turned.

So let us gather, in embrace we stand,
With hearts wide open, united hand in hand.
In this grand design, we find our part,
Threads of understanding weave the heart.

Nourished by Compassion

In acts of kindness, seeds are sown,
In hearts of many, compassion's grown.
With every gesture, a bond is made,
In love's embrace, all fear will fade.

Through helping hands, we stand as one,
Lighting the darkness, just like the sun.
In every smile, in every tear,
Compassion nurtures, we hold dear.

Through trials faced, we learn to care,
In the depth of struggle, we find our share.
Together we rise, together we fight,
Nourished by compassion, we find the light.

Let hearts expand, let voices ring,
In the song of hope, let us all sing.
Through every challenge that comes our way,
Compassion sustains, come what may.

So here's to the love, to the warmth we give,
In compassionate acts, together we live.
With open hearts, let's pave the path,
Nourished by compassion, we embrace the laugh.

Blending Experiences

In twilight's soft embrace we meet,
Stories shared, with laughter sweet.
A tapestry of lives we weave,
In moments lived, we dare believe.

From different paths we journey came,
With open hearts and no shame.
Each tale a thread, each joy a spark,
In the hearth's glow, we leave our mark.

The fusion of our dreams takes flight,
Through shared whispers in the night.
With every echo, bonds grow tight,
In this dance, we find our light.

Colors blend beneath the stars,
Erasing distance, mending scars.
In this union of souls, we find,
A gentle warmth that soothes the mind.

Together, we create a rhyme,
Capturing the essence of time.
In the tapestry of night and day,
We find our peace, we find our way.

Gathering around the Table

Around the table, hearts align,
With every dish, a taste divine.
Laughter mingles with the feast,
In simple joy, our love released.

Stories shared with every bite,
Remembrances of pure delight.
The clinking glasses raise a cheer,
In these moments, we draw near.

Each seat filled with warmth and grace,
In this haven, we find our place.
With every smile, the world feels right,
The table set, a sacred sight.

Conversations flow like wine,
In the glow of candle shine.
As dishes pass, so too our dreams,
We gather close, or so it seems.

Through shared meals, we stitch our fate,
Building bonds that won't abate.
Around the table, love does bloom,
In every corner, joy assumes.

The Undercurrent of Trust

Beneath the surface, we explore,
An unseen link, a steady shore.
In whispered truths, our hearts connect,
In vulnerability, we reflect.

Through storms and trials, hand in hand,
We navigate, we understand.
The silent promises we weave,
In every moment, we believe.

Eyes that speak without a word,
In every glance, our thoughts are heard.
Through trials faced, and laughter shared,
In this bond, our hearts are bared.

The undertone of faith runs deep,
In quiet nights, when dreams won't sleep.
A flow of trust that can't be seen,
In every setback, we lean clean.

In the tapestry of our days,
We find strength in the subtlest ways.
With threads of trust, together we bind,
Creating a bond, unconfined.

Milestones of Togetherness

Each milestone marks a journey's end,
With laughter, love, and time to spend.
In every corner, memories grow,
A cherished place where feelings flow.

Celebrated days, both big and small,
In this circle, we embrace it all.
From first steps to the vows we take,
We honor paths that we all make.

With candles lit and wishes made,
In unity, fears will fade.
A tapestry of moments bright,
In every shadow, there's still light.

Reflecting on the paths we've crossed,
In every gain, we count no loss.
With hands held high, we face the dawn,
In milestones passed, we are reborn.

Through seasons change, our roots run deep,
In shared laughter, we shall keep.
Together, we'll chart the unknown way,
In milestones marked, come what may.

Infusing Humor

Laughter dances in the air,
Tickling hearts without a care.
A joke exchanged, a smile wide,
In humor's glow, we all abide.

Wit and whimsy sprinkle the day,
Turning mundane into a play.
With every giggle, worries fade,
In laughter's light, our fears delayed.

Sarcasm wrapped in gentle cheer,
Bringing friends and strangers near.
We share the joy, we bridge the gap,
In chuckles, we find our happy map.

Jests and tales, a playful blend,
In every snicker, we transcend.
Through ups and downs, we find our tune,
In humor's arms, we feel immune.

So let us toast to laughter bright,
That warms our souls and sparks delight.
For in this life, let's make it clear,
Humor holds the magic here.

Sturdy Foundations

A solid base to start anew,
Trust entwined, in all we do.
Brick by brick, we build and rise,
With sturdy roots, we touch the skies.

Through storms that shake and winds that howl,
Our bonds will last, we've made a vow.
In every challenge, hand in hand,
We find our strength, we take a stand.

Each sturdy beam, a tale we share,
In engaged hearts, we sow our care.
A place of warmth, where love can grow,
In steadfast hearts, our hopes will flow.

With patience strong and laughter bright,
We cultivate our dreams in sight.
No cracks can break what's built with love,
Our sturdy bond, a gift from above.

So here's to roots that intertwine,
In every season, bright and fine.
Foundations laid, forever true,
In sturdy hearts, we'll see it through.

The Craft of Companionship

In every moment, side by side,
With open hearts, our joys abide.
Through laughter shared, and whispers soft,
In companionship, we soar aloft.

We paint our days with colors bold,
Stories woven with threads of gold.
In each embrace, warmth fills the air,
A quiet strength, in loving care.

From simple chats to dreams we'll chase,
In every hug, we find our place.
Supporting hands, as seasons change,
In companionship, we rearrange.

With patience learned, and trust bestowed,
We walk the path, the love we showed.
In every step, together we'll tread,
A tapestry of words unsaid.

So here's to all the bonds we share,
In every trial, we'll always care.
The craft of friendship, a precious art,
Forever etched within the heart.

The Taste of Togetherness

Gathered round the table wide,
With cherished friends, our hearts collide.
The feast laid out, each dish a dream,
In flavors rich, friendships beam.

Each bite a story, shared and sweet,
With laughter mingling, hearts skip a beat.
In sips of joy, we toast the night,
In the taste of love, everything feels right.

Hands reach out for what we crave,
In every meal, connections brave.
From savory to sweets, we explore,
In togetherness, we find much more.

Moments captured with every taste,
No hurried pace, just love embraced.
In every flavor, bonds will grow,
The taste of togetherness, a golden glow.

So let's gather close, let's break the bread,
In the warmth of hearts, our paths are led.
With every meal, we share our bliss,
In the flavor of love, we find our kiss.

The Sweetness of Sacrifice

In twilight's calm, the heart does yearn,
For love that gives, for lessons learned.
The candle burns with gentle grace,
A reminder of each warm embrace.

With open hands, we offer all,
Through bitter times, we hear the call.
For every tear that stains the ground,
New roots of strength will soon be found.

We linger long where shadows play,
To find the light within the fray.
Though journeys steep and paths unclear,
We rise anew with every tear.

In every loss, a seed is sown,
In sacrifice, our courage grown.
For those we cherish, we'll endure,
In giving love, our souls feel pure.

So guard the heart with tender care,
In every deed, the truth we share.
The sweetness found in what we give,
Is in the love that helps us live.

Culinary Comforts of Care

The kitchen warms as memories rise,
With simmering pots and fragrant pies.
A dash of spice, a pinch of love,
Nourishment sent from above.

A table set with plates so bright,
Gathered hearts, a wondrous sight.
Stories shared like soup in bowls,
Stirring comfort in hungry souls.

From chopping greens to baking bread,
Each meal whispers, "You're well-fed."
The flavors dance, a joyful tune,
In every bite, the love is strewn.

The laughter rolls as children play,
In culinary bliss, we stay.
With every dish shared side by side,
In memories made, we take pride.

So let us feast on life's delight,
In every meal, warmth takes flight.
The culinary comforts we create,
Are love served daily on our plate.

Sprinkling Honesty

A truth unfolds in gentle sighs,
Where words take flight and never lie.
We sprinkle faith like morning dew,
A bond that's strong and beautifully true.

In whispered tones, the heart reveals,
Through honest words, connection feels.
Let every statement ground our roots,
Each word a seed, each thought, a shoot.

Amidst the noise, the purest sound,
In honesty, our hopes are found.
Like silver laces on a shoe,
With every step, we build anew.

No masks to wear, just open hearts,
In vulnerability, truth imparts.
With every glance, in every chance,
We find the strength in honest dance.

So let us share, let us be free,
With words that flow like a clear sea.
In sprinkling truth, we come alive,
With every moment, we will thrive.

Building Bridges with Ingredients

A dash of kindness, a slice of grace,
In every kitchen, we find our place.
We gather flavors from far and wide,
Building bridges as we stir inside.

From cultures rich, our plates adorned,
In unity, our hearts are warmed.
With every spice and every zest,
We find in food, a shared quest.

The art of cooking, a timeless thread,
In every meal, new paths are spread.
As dishes blend, so do our souls,
In food's embrace, we find our goals.

So chop and dice, let laughter soar,
Through culinary, we explore.
Each ingredient, a tale to tell,
In every taste, our friendship swells.

Together we forge, together we bake,
With love and care, the world we make.
In kitchens bright, our spirits sing,
Building bridges, the joy we bring.

Celebrating Differences

In every shade, a story blooms,
Each voice a note in life's grand tune.
Together we weave our tapestry,
In the threads of unity, we find harmony.

Different paths, yet hearts align,
Cultures rich, and spirits shine.
Hand in hand, we dance as one,
In diversity, our strengths are spun.

Stars above, both bright and small,
Illuminate the night for all.
Embracing gaps, we stand as friends,
In the beauty of our blend, love transcends.

Voices rise, a vibrant choir,
Each note unique, yet all aspire.
To celebrate what makes us whole,
In every difference, we find our soul.

Together we stand, never apart,
Unity thrives in every heart.
Together we shine, forever bold,
In our differences, true beauty unfolds.

A Potpourri of Perspectives

A canvas painted with different hues,
Each stroke a thought, diverse views.
In a world of contrast, we see the light,
From each angle, a view so bright.

Ideas collide, sparks ignite,
In the dance of minds, we take flight.
Every word, a seed that's sown,
From many roots, our thoughts have grown.

Listen closely, the whispers soar,
In each silence, there's so much more.
Beyond borders, we share our dreams,
A tapestry woven with golden seams.

Exchange of thoughts, a gentle breeze,
Bringing together, what love frees.
United in wonder, we venture forth,
In a potpourri of minds, our worth.

Voices echo, wisdom flows,
In the beauty of difference, truth glows.
Together we flourish, bloom through storms,
In this rich mosaic, our spirit warms.

Buttering Up Compassion

A kind word softly spreads its wings,
Nurturing hearts, as warmth it brings.
Like butter melting on fresh bread,
Compassion blooms where love is spread.

Tender smiles, an open door,
In quiet moments, we learn much more.
Listening deep, with hearts attuned,
In the silence, friendships are honed.

Acts of kindness, small but bold,
In every gesture, a story told.
We gather around, share our part,
With every touch, we warm the heart.

A gentle nudge, a helping hand,
In simple moments, we understand.
We rise together, through joy and pain,
In compassion's embrace, life we gain.

So let us weave with threads of grace,
Creating joy in every space.
With love as our guide, let's lift the veil,
In a world of compassion, we shall prevail.

Cracking Open Conversations

Let's crack the shell and take a look,
Start the dialogue with one small hook.
In simple words, we find the way,
To share our thoughts, come what may.

Open hearts and minds set free,
In every exchange, a mystery.
With every question, we break the ice,
In conversations, we find our spice.

Storytelling flows, like rivers wide,
In shared experiences, we confide.
Release the doubts, let voices ring,
In every conversation, new hope can spring.

Listen deeply, cherish the share,
In each connection, we show we care.
Let laughter linger, and stories unfold,
In every narrative, a glimpse of gold.

Together we bloom, through every chat,
Through differences, we find where we're at.
So crack open life, take a chance,
In the rhythm of dialogue, we dance.

Recipes for Lasting Love

In the kitchen where hearts align,
A sprinkle of trust, a dash of time,
Mix laughter with whispers, sweet delight,
Bake memories together, warm and bright.

Stir patience in a simmering pot,
Season with kindness, give it a shot,
Serve it up warm on a silver plate,
Pour joy like wine, let it elevate.

Knead bonds together, firm and strong,
Let passion rise, it won't take long,
Taste the essence that love can bring,
Feel the rhythm, let your hearts sing.

With every recipe, share your dreams,
In the fondue pot, fate gently steams,
A pinch of hope, a splash of care,
Savor the moments, together you share.

Love simmers slowly, rich and profound,
In a banquet of feelings, always abound,
Set the table with joy, never fear,
For lasting love's feast, year after year.

Stirring the Soul

In quiet moments, find your pause,
Let stillness whisper, without a cause,
Awaken the spirit, let it unfold,
As warmth ignites the heart, uncontrolled.

Breathe in the beauty of life's sweet song,
Dance with the rhythm, where you belong,
Each heartbeat a melody, soft and pure,
Stirring the soul, vibrant and sure.

Wander through whispers of the night,
Feel the world's canvas, painted bright,
Explore the depths of your inner well,
In silence, the truth has stories to tell.

Awaken your senses, let passion ignite,
With every small spark, turn darkness to light,
Stirring the soul, let the journey begin,
For within every ending lies another win.

Embrace each challenge, learn and evolve,
Turn chaos to calm, and let love resolve,
In the pot of existence, let peace take its toll,
For life is a journey, stirring the soul.

Savoring Shared Moments

In the warmth of daylight, laughter rings,
Capturing joy in the simplest things,
A shared glance, a touch, a gentle sigh,
Moments that linger, like stars in the sky.

With every sunrise, paint feelings anew,
Gather the essence, just me and you,
In the tapestry of time, we weave,
Savoring shared moments, hearts on our sleeves.

Like breadcrumbs left on a winding path,
Discover the treasures, avoid the wrath,
In memories gathered, we find our way,
Savoring the seconds, day by day.

With each heartbeat, cherish the now,
Cultivate kindness, let love take a bow,
In the garden of trust, let's plant our dreams,
Savor these moments, or so it seems.

As evening draws close, we reminisce,
Counting the moments, it's pure bliss,
Together we gather, like fireflies' glow,
Savoring shared moments, watching love grow.

A Platform of Respect

In the meeting of minds, we stand tall,
Building foundations where heartbeats call,
With open ears and gentle grace,
Creating a space where all have a place.

Let voices be heard, loud and clear,
In the chorus of dialogue, hold it dear,
With kindness as armor, we learn to agree,
In the platform of respect, we strive to be.

Diverse minds unite, hand in hand,
Together we flourish, together we stand,
Each story a thread in the fabric of time,
In the tapestry woven with wisdom, we climb.

Celebrate differences, embrace what's unique,
In the heart of the matter, let's softly speak,
For in every connection, a lesson unfolds,
A platform of respect is where love molds.

With courage and grace, let us walk the line,
For unity blossoms when respect intertwines,
In this sacred space, let's journey as one,
In the platform of respect, we rise with the sun.

Simmering Shades of Support

In twilight's calm, we stand as one,
With hearts aflame, our journey begun.
Each whispered word, a gentle balm,
Together we bloom, in grace and calm.

Through storms we weather, clouds may roll,
But hands entwined, we stay whole.
A bridge of trust, forever near,
In shadows dim, your light draws clear.

Like autumn leaves, we softly fall,
In unity, we rise and call.
Support like roots, deep and wide,
In every struggle, side by side.

With every challenge, joy unfolds,
In shared moments, love beholds.
Through laughter shared and tears that gleam,
Together we weave, a vivid dream.

Boiling Points and Breakthroughs

In bubbling pots, ideas ignite,
Fierce with passion, sharp as light.
Pressure builds, like a storm within,
A spark of change, where hope begins.

Through trials tough, we push through pain,
In every struggle, wisdom gained.
With boiling hearts, we dare to leap,
Transforming depths, no time for sleep.

When cracks appear, don't shy away,
In fractured silence, truths will sway.
We find the strength, let courage speak,
From moments weak, our futures peak.

With every challenge that we embrace,
We forge ahead, we find our place.
In boiling points, we rise anew,
Through pain and joy, we push on through.

Seasons of Shared Growth

In springtime blooms, our hopes arise,
With petals soft, beneath clear skies.
We nurture dreams, like tender seeds,
In unity, we meet our needs.

Summer sun, we bask in light,
With laughter bright, the world feels right.
Together we dance, in warmth and cheer,
In seasons shared, our hearts sincere.

As autumn leaves begin to fall,
We gather strength, we heed the call.
In changing tides, we find our way,
With gratitude, we greet the day.

In winter's chill, we huddle close,
With stories shared, it's you I chose.
Through frost and snow, our bonds grow tight,
In every season, we shine so bright.

A Pinch of Patience

In time's embrace, we learn to wait,
A dash of hope on every plate.
With gentle hands, we mold our fate,
In patience found, we celebrate.

With every heartbeat, moments blend,
In slowing down, we start to mend.
A sprinkle of faith in all we do,
Brings forth the strength to push on through.

As seasons shift and daylight fades,
We find the peace in quieter glades.
Each quiet step, a soft caress,
In patience, true, we find success.

With whispers low, we tread the path,
In every trial, we learn to laugh.
A pinch of patience, we hold dear,
Guiding us onward, year by year.

The Blend of Diversity

In colors rich, we come alive,
With voices strong, we learn to thrive.
Each difference shines, a vibrant spark,
Together we light up the dark.

From cultures mixed, we share our tales,
In unity, our spirit sails.
With open hearts, we bridge the gap,
In diversity, we find our map.

Each flavor adds a special touch,
In harmony, we blend so much.
We celebrate in joyful dance,
A world reborn, a second chance.

Through different paths, our journeys merge,
In every heartbeat, passions surge.
Embrace the unique, let kindness flow,
From diversity, together we grow.

Let kindness guide, let love extend,
In every hand, a willing friend.
The blend of us, a masterpiece,
In unity, we find our peace.

Unbreakable Façades

Behind the smiles, the hidden fears,
A world of pain, suppressed by years.
We wear our masks, through day and night,
Yet inside us burns a hopeful light.

The faces change, but truths reside,
In whispered thoughts, where doubts confide.
We guard our hearts with walls so tall,
Yet beneath the surface, we yearn to call.

Through storms we stand, through trials we press,
The shadows linger, but we express.
In silent battles, we fight alone,
Yet strength, like roots, is deeply sown.

The façade may shield what we can't share,
But in every crack, hope finds its air.
With each authentic word we let fall,
We break the silence, we break the wall.

Unseen, unheard, we find our way,
Through shattered dreams, we learn to stay.
In every truth, in every scar,
We rise resilient, we love from afar.

A Tapestry of Support

In threads so fine, our stories weave,
A tapestry strong, we all believe.
Each strand unique, yet intertwined,
In strength combined, our spirits aligned.

Through trials faced, we stand our ground,
In whispered hopes, support is found.
With every gesture, big or small,
Together we rise, we will not fall.

Like colors bright against a grey,
We lift each other, come what may.
In moments dark, a light we share,
A fabric woven with genuine care.

We stitch our dreams in patterns bold,
In every heart, a story told.
The bonds we form are rich and deep,
In unity, our vigil we keep.

A tapestry made of laughter and tears,
In every thread, we conquer fears.
With open hearts, we build and mend,
A tapestry of support that will not end.

Garnishing with Gratitude

In every dawn, new chances bloom,
With grateful hearts, we chase the gloom.
Each moment sweet, a chance to see,
The gifts of life, a symphony.

With every friend, a treasure gained,
In shared laughter, no joy is drained.
We lift each other, hand in hand,
In gratitude's glow, together we stand.

Through seasons change, our hearts align,
In every struggle, our spirits shine.
For every lesson, both hard and true,
We garnish life with appreciation too.

The simple things, they mean the most,
In every smile, we raise a toast.
With thankful hearts, we seek and find,
The beauty in life, so intertwined.

As sunsets paint the evening skies,
In gratitude, our spirits rise.
To celebrate all we hold dear,
With garnished hearts, we persevere.

Stirring the Pot of Understanding

In the calm of a gentle breeze,
We share our thoughts with ease,
A mix of hearts begins to blend,
In this space, we find a friend.

With each stir, the flavors grow,
A deeper bond begins to flow,
Listening close, we open wide,
Turning tides we must abide.

Spices of hope, a pinch of trust,
In this pot, it's a must,
We learn to see from others' eyes,
In empathy, true wisdom lies.

Every story brings a taste,
Every moment, none to waste,
Stirring slowly, we create,
A better world, there's no debate.

So let us cook, with care and love,
Mixing magic, as if from above,
Stirring the pot, together we rise,
In understanding, the heart complies.

The Secret Sauce of Support

A dash of kindness, a scoop of care,
In each gesture, we learn to share,
The secret sauce, a blend divine,
Helps us shine, our spirits align.

In quiet moments, a hand to hold,
Stories of courage, silently told,
We lift each other, through thick and thin,
Together, we find where strength begins.

Laughter bubbles, like sweet delight,
In the warmth, we find our light,
Each drop of support, a taste so true,
A recipe of love, me and you.

As challenges rise, we stand as one,
In this journey, we come undone,
But with the blend of trust and grace,
We overcome, we find our place.

So pour your heart into the mix,
A secret sauce that truly sticks,
In unity, we savor the blend,
Support is the key that never ends.

Nurtured by Listening

In the garden of our shared thoughts,
Listening deeply, wisdom is sought,
Each word a seed, in silence they bloom,
Creating a space where we find room.

With open ears and open hearts,
We cultivate trust, where kindness starts,
In every story, we find a place,
Nurtured by grace, we embrace.

The gentle art of holding space,
Each heartbeat a slow, steady pace,
Moments shared, like roots entwined,
In this bond, connections refined.

Through the whispers, and through the sighs,
We gain strength from our allies,
In these exchanges, we find a way,
A garden of hope, where we can stay.

So let us listen, let us grow,
In the light of love's gentle glow,
For in each voice, a story's told,
Nurtured by listening, brave and bold.

A Dash of Forgiveness

In the heart where grudges lay,
A dash of forgiveness finds its way,
Like a balm for wounds, so deep,
It offers peace, a chance to leap.

When shadows linger, we choose to shine,
In letting go, the stars align,
With every act of kind release,
We find our way to inner peace.

Words unsaid, and actions past,
The art of healing holds us fast,
A sprinkle of grace, a gentle sigh,
Transforms the pain, allows us to fly.

With each breath, we let it mend,
In this journey, we need to bend,
A dash of forgiveness, a life to mend,
In the tapestry of love, we ascend.

So let us rise, together we stand,
A sprinkle of hope, a guiding hand,
With forgiveness as our sacred fire,
We build anew, we rise ever higher.

Mixture of Acceptance

In shadows deep, we find our way,
A dance of truth in light of day.
With open hearts, we greet the new,
Embracing flaws that make us true.

The mirror shows a world so vast,
Each story shared, a future cast.
We blend our dreams, both bright and dim,
In unity, we learn to swim.

The warmth of hands, together strong,
In every note, we share a song.
Through trials faced, we lift the veil,
In courage found, we'll never fail.

A tapestry of shades we weave,
In every thread, we choose to believe.
Step by step, we rise and stand,
Acceptance blooms from every hand.

With every heartbeat, we'll embrace,
The beauty found in every place.
Together we can weather storms,
In acceptance, our spirit warms.

Flourishing in Harmony

In gentle whispers, nature speaks,
A symphony that softly seeks.
Each leaf that rustles, each bird that sings,
Together loud, our spirit brings.

The river flows with grace untold,
Embracing warmth against the cold.
Among the branches, light will play,
In harmony, we find our way.

Colors merge in vibrant waves,
Each heart entwined, the spirit saves.
We share the sun, the moon, the stars,
No longer bound by distant bars.

In unity, we plant our seeds,
Nurturing through each other's needs.
In gardens rich, we grow and bloom,
With love and care, we banish gloom.

The world a canvas painted bright,
In every hue, we find our light.
Together, hand in hand, we stand,
Flourishing in this vast land.

A Dash of Forgiveness

In whispered sighs, we lay our ghosts,
Releasing burdens, healing most.
Forgiveness found in tender grace,
We find the strength to face each place.

The heart, so heavy, starts to mend,
In kindness shown, we start to blend.
Letting go of all that's past,
In gentle waves, we find our cast.

Each step we take, a chance to heal,
To bridge the gaps, our truth reveal.
In open arms, we seek to grow,
A dash of love, a healing flow.

The scars we wear, a badge of pride,
In every story, we can hide.
Yet in the light of truth so clear,
Forgiveness blooms, dispelling fear.

With every tear, a seed we plant,
In fertile ground, our spirits chant.
Through love and trust, we break the chains,
Forgiveness, sweet, through all remains.

Whisking Away Doubts

In morning light, we face the day,
With dreams to chase and fears to sway.
Each thought, a whisper in the air,
We rise like bread, beyond despair.

A gentle hand, we stir the pot,
Creating magic from what we've got.
With every twist, we shape our fate,
Whisking away what feels too late.

The doubts may knock upon our door,
Yet courage waits, an open store.
To taste our strength in every bite,
We find our way, our hearts ignite.

Embracing change with each new blend,
In every choice, we transcend.
Through trials faced, we learn to trust,
Whisking away fears into dust.

The recipe of life unfolds,
With flavors rich and tales retold.
Together, we can face it all,
In unity, we shall not fall.

Heartstrings and Hearthstones

In the glow of soft lamplight,
We gather close and share our dreams,
Laughter spins through the night air,
Embracing warmth in shared beams.

Each heartbeat echoes a story,
A thread that ties us, firm and strong,
Through trials faced and fleeting glory,
Together we find where we belong.

With every word, we weave our fate,
Drawing comfort from tender threads,
Building a haven, never late,
In heart's embrace, our fear sheds.

The music of voices intertwined,
Creates a tapestry, bright and bold,
In unity, our souls aligned,
A masterpiece of warmth to hold.

So let the hearthstones ever blaze,
In memories made, our love ignites,
With heartstrings tethered in a maze,
Together we journey toward new heights.

Bonds Forged in Kindness

In whispers soft, we share our fears,
A hand to hold, a gentle touch,
Through every storm, through all the years,
It's kindness that has meant so much.

A smile exchanged, a gesture small,
Can lift the weight from weary minds,
In simple acts, we rise or fall,
In bonds of love, our heart entwines.

Through trials faced and laughter shared,
We find a strength we never knew,
In kindness shown, we are bared,
Each deed reflecting the love that grew.

When shadows loom and doubts arise,
We stand as one, hand in hand,
For in these moments, hope defies,
With kindness, together we will stand.

These bonds we forge are made of gold,
In every heart, this truth is clear,
Through kindness shared, love unfolds,
And after storms, we always cheer.

Ingredients of Togetherness

A pinch of laughter, a dash of care,
Mixing memories as we combine,
Cooking stories that we all share,
In the kitchen, love's pure design.

A sprinkle of joy, a savor of trust,
Stirring flavors that dance and blend,
In every dish, a bond robust,
With every meal, we find a friend.

With arms around the table wide,
We savor moments, taste and feel,
In every bite, our hearts abide,
Creating warmth, a hearty meal.

As seasons change, so does our feast,
Each gathering an endless spread,
In each creation, joy increased,
Together, in memories, we're fed.

So here's to love, our secret spice,
To every meal shared in delight,
With ingredients of laughter and nice,
Together we shine, our hearts alight.

Whispers of Trust

In quiet moments, secrets shared,
The weight of silence speaks so loud,
With every whisper, love is bared,
A bond unbroken, strong and proud.

Through trials faced, we find our way,
In whispered hopes that breathe and flow,
As shadows gather, come what may,
Our trust ignites an inner glow.

Fingers woven, touching souls,
In every word, a promise made,
In this connection, time unrolls,
With gentle hearts, we are not frayed.

So when the night grows dark and cold,
In whispered trust, we find the light,
With every story, love unfolds,
Together facing every fight.

It's in these whispers, hearts entwined,
A tapestry of faith we weave,
In trust, a treasure, rare to find,
In every breath, together breathe.

Measuring Moments of Joy

In laughter shared and stories told,
We find the warmth against the cold.
Each smile a memory, a spark of light,
Moments of joy, so pure, so bright.

With every sunset, colors blend,
We savor the time spent with a friend.
Each fleeting glance, a heart's embrace,
Joy's measure found in this sacred space.

The sound of giggles fills the air,
A treasure trove of memories rare.
In simple things, our hearts take flight,
Moments of joy, our souls' delight.

Like raindrops falling on thirsty ground,
In moments cherished, love is found.
Each heartbeat echoes, a rhythmic song,
In this dance of life, we all belong.

So gather close, let laughter ring,
For every joy, a new song to sing.
In measuring moments, we encourage grace,
In every heartbeat, a loving embrace.

Growth in the Garden of Friendship

In the garden where secrets bloom,
Friendship flourishes, dispelling gloom.
With roots entwined beneath the earth,
Together we nurture our shared worth.

Each laughter sown, a seedling's start,
Watered with trust, we nurture the heart.
Through seasons changing, we endure,
In this garden, our bond grows pure.

Sunshine and shadows, both play their part,
We celebrate growth; we heal, we start.
With petals soft, in colors bold,
Friendship's beauty, a story told.

In the twilight's glow, we gather near,
Planting our dreams without fear.
Through storms that may test our steady ground,
In the garden of friendship, love is found.

So tend to the blooms, and cherish the vines,
In the garden of life, our true love shines.
With every heartbeat, with every sigh,
In this sacred space, our spirits fly.

Layers of Love

In the warmth of a gentle touch,
We find layers of love, oh so much.
With whispers soft, secrets exchange,
Each layer unfurls, beautifully strange.

Through time and trials, we learn and grow,
In every heartbeat, our love's gentle flow.
A tapestry woven with threads of care,
In layers of love, we lay ourselves bare.

In laughter's echo, in silence shared,
Each moment cherished, each soul laid bare.
In the depths of connection, we do find
The layers of love that bind heart and mind.

With every sunrise, new depths unfold,
Layers of warmth, more precious than gold.
In the journey together, we write our song,
In this dance of love, we both belong.

So here's to the layers, both thin and thick,
In every heartbeat, love's magic will stick.
Bound in the journey that time cannot sever,
With layers of love, we'll flourish forever.

The Flavor of Forgiveness

In the heart's pantry lies a key,
The flavor of forgiveness, wild and free.
With spices of courage, and salt of tears,
We blend our sorrows, quiet our fears.

A dash of patience, a sprinkle of grace,
Each bite of healing finds its place.
In tender moments where hearts unite,
The flavor of forgiveness, pure delight.

With every gesture, a recipe shared,
Simmering warmth shows how we cared.
In the kitchen of life, we stir and create,
The flavor of forgiveness helps us relate.

Through open hearts, we learn to mend,
In the scent of love, our wounds transcend.
With every taste, bitterness grows small,
The flavor of forgiveness, it conquers all.

So let us savor the moments divine,
With flavors that linger, hearts intertwine.
In this feast of life, let us find space,
For the flavor of forgiveness, a warm embrace.

Milton Keynes UK
Ingram Content Group UK Ltd.
UKHW022142111124
451073UK00007B/156